CHRISTOPHER RAJA migrated from Calcutta to Melbourne in 1986, and almost twenty years later he moved again, further inland, living and working in Alice Springs since 2004. Chris was co-guest consultant editor of *Meanjin*'s Australasian issue in 2004 and since then has been a regular contributor to *Meanjin*, *Quadrant*, *Southerly* and *Art Monthly Australia*. His short story 'After the Wreck' was adapted for radio and broadcast on ABC Radio National's Short Story Program in 2007. His play *Drew's Seizure* was performed at Araluen Arts Centre, Alice Springs in 2009. Chris worked as the NT Correspondent for *Art Monthly Australia* from 2010 to 2011 and he is currently a History and English teacher at St Philip's College, Alice Springs. He and his actor wife Natasha co-wrote *The First Garden*, with the assistance of a grant from Arts NT, which premiered in September 2011 and played over six nights at the Olive Pink Botanic Garden. Chris co-curated 'Art of the Nomads' at the Chan Contemporary Art Space in Darwin in April 2012. He was selected for the Australian Society of Authors 2011/2012 mentorship program. His novel *The Burning Elephant* is represented by The Colchie Agency and A Wyatt Book, Inc.

NATASHA RAJA was born in Port Adelaide in 1984 and began performing shortly thereafter. In 2000 Natasha moved to Alice Springs and continued to perform at local events. After matriculation, she spent five years looking after the elderly and disabled in town and on remote communities in the APY lands and Yuendumu. In 2007 the birth of her daughter Harper inspired Natasha to embark on a creative journey. She coordinated Alice Springs' first short play festival 'Bite Sized Theatre' in which she also played Eric, a precocious embryo. Natasha has been the dulcet voice of Wearable Arts for the past four years. In 2010 she was Jill Tanner in the production *Butterflies Are Free*' More recently she has encouraged her husband Chris to get involved in theatre and together, whilst waiting for the arrival of their daughter Jala, they wrote *The First Garden*.

Eshua Bolton (left) as Johnny, Scott Fraser (background) as Harold and Natasha Raja as Olive in the 2011 Alice Desert Festival production at the Olive Pink Botanic Garden in Alice Springs. (Photo: Steven Pearce)

THE FIRST GARDEN

CHRISTOPHER RAJA & NATASHA RAJA

CURRENCY PLAYS

First published in 2012
by Currency Press Pty Ltd,
PO Box 2287, Strawberry Hills, NSW, 2012, Australia
enquiries@currency.com.au
www.currency.com.au

NATIONAL LIBRARY OF AUSTRALIA CIP DATA

Author: Raja, Christopher.
Title: The first garden / Christopher and Natasha Raja.
ISBN: 9780868199474 (pbk.)
Subjects: Pink, Olive M.—Drama.
                  Environmentalists—Northern Territory—Drama.
                  Lobbying—Northern Territory—Drama.
Other Authors/Contributors:
                  Raja, Natasha.
Dewey Number: A822.4

The First Garden was created with assistance from the Commonwealth Government through the Australia Council, its arts funding and advisory body.

Australian Government

Australia Council
for the Arts

Contents

Typeset by Dean Nottle for Currency Press.
Cover design by Katy Wall for Currency Press.
Front cover shows Natasha Raja as Olive in the 2011 Alice Desert Festival
production at the Olive Pink Botanic Garden in Alice Springs (Photo: Steven
Pearce).
Currency Press acknowledges the Traditional Owners of the Country on
which we live and work. We pay our respects to all Aboriginal and Torres
Strait Islander Elders, past and present.

Scott Fraser as Henry in the 2011 Alice Desert Festival production at the Olive Pink Botanic Garden in Alice Springs. (Photo: Steven Pearce)

INTRODUCTION

When I commenced in the role as Curator of the Olive Pink Botanic Garden in Alice Springs three years ago I was unaware of the notoriety of the garden's namesake, Miss Olive Muriel Pink. As I began to glean insight into her remarkable life, I was presented with an iconic story of a woman's struggle to voice the plight of the first Australians, long before the modern human rights movement.

The popular myth surrounding Miss Pink painted her as an eccentric old woman, bitter and dismissive of the world in which she lived. She was ridiculed by her peers and shunned by the community for espousing ideals that were considered to be outlandish. In the town of Alice Springs she was viewed as a public nuisance, to be tolerated, but barely.

The First Garden challenges this flawed story. The themes of the work touch on key narratives in modern Australian identity, seamlessly incorporating Aboriginal rights, environmentalism, the Gallipoli legend and feminism into its gentle rhythmic tone. This reflects a maturation of our society, where we are prepared not only to acknowledge but also to reconcile.

The archetypal characters depicted—Miss Pink the Martyr, Tjampitjimpa the Wise Man, Harold the Fallen Soldier, Tasman the Lost Boy and Henry the Messenger—relate their stories through gentle sophisticated dialogue and excerpts from Miss Pink's historical letters. These relationships ultimately explore the dispossession of people's rights to land and cultural practice.

One of Alice Springs' custodians, Auntie Doris Stuart—Apmereke Artweye for Mparntwe, the Arrernte name for the town—has shared her insights into Miss Pink's story and the persecutions faced in central Australia. Though Miss Pink and Auntie Doris were never friends—in fact there was as much fear of Miss Pink in the Aboriginal community as the European—there was a deep reciprocated respect. Over several mornings spent with Auntie Doris sipping cups of tea, listening intently and slowly, I began to understand the factors that had so inspired Miss Pink.

Central Australia is a place where modern Western society, in what may be the world's richest nation, coexists alongside the oldest culture on earth. The vast remoteness of the interior and an extraordinary knowledge of this landscape, refined over tens of thousands of years, have ensured that a most ancient culture has survived to this day. The knife-edge nature of life in the desert requires that people from this land live by sympathetic understanding of their surroundings. Our modern society is yet to grasp this fundamental lesson.

The complex belief systems that have been developed for this place encapsulate the plants, the animals, the rocks and the seasons, providing a framework for survival and environmental management. The First Australians were caretakers and custodians, a role duly adopted by Miss Pink in founding the Botanic Garden.

Auntie Doris represents one of the keenest intellects that I have had the pleasure to come to know. She is an embodiment of perseverance in the face of adversity, and a living reminder of the best qualities of Miss Olive Pink. Her knowledge and ability to move between worlds provides a bridge, demonstrating the ability of two cultures to coexist and giving hope for the future of all the people of Central Australia.

On the opening night, of the first season of *The First Garden*, Doris Stuart shared a heartfelt truth which I would like you to read and hold with you as you enjoy this work by Chris and Natasha Raja.

Benjamin Convery
Olive Pink Botanic Garden
Alice Springs, NT
March 2012

Benjamin Convery is the Curator at Olive Pink Botanic Garden.

* * * * *

My Country

Hello everyone. My name is Doris Stuart.

Stuart... this was the name of my father and his father before that... This is our name because this is our country... Stuart was the name this place was given by the incoming Europeans in the late 1800s. That lasted until 1932... maybe 50 years?

Then the name of this place changed to Alice Springs... the name Europeans gave a spring, an important place a little way north of this spot. The place on the river where they built the telegraph station...

But this place we call Alice Springs has another name... Mparntwe... that is what this place you all call Alice Springs was named long before you all came here, and it still is. I am Apmereke Artweye for Mparntwe... this is where I come from... This is my country. We're from here... Apmereke Artweye—custodians for this country.

Welcome to country. It sounds easy, doesn't it? You acknowledge the authority of registered Native Title holders, such as myself. I greet you all, and I welcome you all in response and we all feel good... But in truth it's a little more complicated than that.

I tried to explain that when I was a child, not so long ago, and for all time before that, people couldn't just walk into Mparntwe uninvited. They had to sit down at certain boundaries, places such as Ntaripe— The Gap as you all know it—they had to sit down and ask permission of the Apmereke Artweye to enter Mparntwe, and they knew they might be told they weren't welcome.

It was a bit like you would expect strangers to knock at your door and wait to be invited in, rather than just walking into your home. During that discussion, my friend explained that 'Welcome to Country' was practised by organisations as a positive and respectful activity—an acknowledgement of that invisible front door and Aboriginal custodians' rights to control who walked through it.

My sister and I explained that these 'Welcomes' didn't really feel reasonable to us because the truth was that if you all knock we are simply expected to open our door and say welcome. It's a ritual that doesn't always make us feel respected... it doesn't necessarily leave us feeling like our voices have been heard. Can we actually say no? You're not welcome? We can't... you are all here already.

So, given the complexities of this particular discussion with dear friends, we arrived at a more satisfactory declaration. The one thing we all agreed on was that an 'Acknowledgement of Country' would feel more appropriate.

So I ask you all to take a moment and join me in Acknowledging this Country and all that it gives us every day that we are here. And I want to thank you all for listening to my words.'

Doris Stuart / Apmereke Artweye
Mparntwe
17 September 2011

* * * * *

The First Garden was first produced by Alice Desert Festival, Central Australian Producers Program at the Olive Pink Botanic Garden, Alice Springs, on 17 September 2011 with the following cast:

OLIVE	Natasha Raja
JOHNNY / TASMAN	Eshua Bolton
HAROLD / HENRY	Scott Fraser

Director, Steve Kidd
Designer, Kristina Kidd
Dramaturg, Peter Matheson
Musical Director, Christopher Brocklebank
Technical Director, Kallum Wilkinson
Production Manager, Kirryn Wilkinson
Producers, Ben Convery, Scott Large, Sima Koether
Marketing Manager, Andrew Raphael
Graphic Design, Rowan Martin
Musicians, Christopher Brocklebank, Nick Raymond, Bill Peechy

ACKNOWLEDGEMENTS

Professor Julie Marcus, *The Indomitable Miss Pink, A Life in Anthropology*, Doris Stuart Kngwarraye, Harry Nelson Jakamarra, Valarie Martin Napaljari, Arts NT, Alice Desert Festival, Red Hot Arts, Wenda Hopkins, Edith Raja, Peter Matheson, Ben Convery, Olive Pink Botanic Garden, Steve Kidd, Kristina Kidd, Kallum Wilkinson, Kirryn Wilkinson, Christopher Brocklebank, Eshua Bolton, Scott Fraser, Steve Pearce, Roger Hammond and Pam Usher.

This play is dedicated to our daughters, Indigo, Harper and Jala.

* * * * *

The Olive Pink Botanic Garden is managed by a not for profit Trust that honours the legacy of its founder Miss Olive Muriel Pink. The garden today is a dynamic space, which actively contributes to the environment and community. The garden presents and produces a diverse program of Arts and Cultural events and works with disadvantaged peoples. The Olive Pink Botanic Garden has been generously supported by private benefactors and philanthropists, corporations and business as well as Federal, State and Local governments.

CHARACTERS

OLIVE PINK: In October 1956, Olive Muriel Pink set up her
tent on the grounds of what is now the Olive Pink Botanical
Garden. From this tranquil location she lobbied NT politicians
vigorously to establish a Flora Reserve to protect native flora
and provide a site where locals could visit and learn about
desert environments. Miss Pink's conflicts with administrators,
missionaries, pastoralists and her anthropological colleagues
are legendary. They often regarded her as an eccentric but
today she can be seen for what she was—a trailblazing
Aboriginal land rights activist and environmentalist.

CAPTAIN HAROLD SOUTHERN: Olive Pink's childhood friend with
whom she was linked romantically and who died on the slopes
of Gallipoli in 1916.

HENRY WARDLAW: Henry was the son of the disapproving
Dr Wardlaw of Sydney University with whom Olive Pink
argued acrimoniously at meetings of the Anthropological
Society of New South Wales. Henry's father is one of Olive's
arch rivals and enemies in Sydney. She was amused to find out
later that Henry was a young communist who wanted to help
Olive. She liked Henry very much.

JOHNNY TJAMPITJINPA: With the help of her friend, Warlpiri
warrior and gardener Johnny Tjampitjinpa, Olive Pink shaped
Australia's first arid zone flora reserve out of a plot of land in
Alice Springs. Tjampitjinpa was a Warlpiri man, naturalist and
gentleman gardener on the Arid Region Flora Reserve for
12 years.

TASMAN: Born at Pirdi Pirdi, Tasman was one of the children
named by Olive Pink.

HAROLD and HENRY are doubled
JOHNNY and TASMAN are doubled.

SETTING

The setting is the Olive Pink Botanic Garden.

Two red river gums form a proscenium. Another red river gum is situated just behind the stage right river gum. The backdrop is the rocks and native plants of the garden. Stage depth is created by numerous native trees. Three plant rows are situated right of centre (from left to right, a row of small red river gums, a row of bean trees and a row of colourful flowers). A functional fireplace consisting of an upside down 44-gallon drum which has been cut to a height of no more than 40 cms as a makeshift stove is at centre stage. An old-style kettle is placed on this. Wood smoke comes from the fire. Stage left is Miss Pink's tent (which is later removed to reveal a rusty tin hut). It is sheltered in the shade of an ironwood tree which is situated to the right of the tent. In front of this ironwood tree is Miss Pink's desk with a chair. On the desk is an old hurricane lamp, leaning on the desk at stage left is a rifle. Rusty eight-gallon drums with non-native flowers in them are scattered around the set. The floor is dirt. A dappled lighting effect illuminates the floor. The light from downstage left spills across the stage moving from late afternoon through twilight to dusk.

Musicians play from behind the audience.

Preset music is playing.

Olive's theme music begins.

OLIVE *walks across the hill into view, carrying a dead goanna. She is dressed in a pith helmet, a white silk blouse tied at the neck, long brown skirt and black lace-up boots.*

As the music fades, OLIVE *addresses the audience in Warlpiri language. Animated and excited.*

OLIVE: *Yuwa nyurdurlaju* [Hey, you mob]! *Purdarnkajurlu* [Listen to me]. *Purnmardarnurna* [I caught a] *wardapi* [goanna]. Over by the *warnirri* [soakage]. *Ngajujurna larnijarijarna* [I was frightened]. I love being out here, in and amongst it. *Wirlyirni.* [Hunting]. If I could live here forever I would.

MAN: [*from offstage*] That one makes good tukka.

OLIVE: Yes. I got him over by the waterhole.

MAN: [*offstage*] Well done. You must go now.

OLIVE: Why? I love it here.

MAN: [*offstage*] You know why. You got to go. You can't stay in this country.

OLIVE: Why have I got to go?

MAN: [*offstage*] You telling whitefellas our business. You got to go.

OLIVE: I am sorry.

MAN: [*offstage*] Go now.

OLIVE: I need time to pack up camp.

MAN: [*offstage*] There's no time. Get yourself out of here!

Olive's theme music returns.

OLIVE *leaves the goanna on a rock and walks down the hill.*

HAROLD *appears from left and follows her down centre stage.*

The music ends.

OLIVE *never looks at* HAROLD *unless scripted.*

OLIVE: Alice Springs is a nauseating place.

HAROLD: It looks dreadful.

OLIVE: It is a modern Sodom and Gomorrah. Full of drink and carry-on.

HAROLD: Precisely.

OLIVE: I've learnt so much about the lives of Aboriginal people.

HAROLD: [*looking at* OLIVE] What on earth led you to this godforsaken place?

OLIVE: Injustice.

HAROLD: What are you going to do here?

He crosses downstage right.

OLIVE: Defend the rights of the Aboriginal people… among other things.

HAROLD: But you are a woman.

OLIVE: I want people to see beyond that.

HAROLD: I am surprised you take notice of what other people see.

OLIVE: I think it's wise to take notice. I want to change white people's behaviour towards the Aborigines.

HAROLD: Change your own behaviour first. I don't think it is wise to poke your nose in here.

OLIVE: The Aborigines placed their trust in this government. They have just turned on them and speared them from behind.

HAROLD: You don't belong here.

OLIVE: It's shameful and degrading how policies are imposed on them.

HAROLD: You sound like a naïve do-gooder.

He crosses stage right.

OLIVE: That's not fair.

HAROLD: No colonisation is fair. Ask the Indians, Africans. It's not supposed to be fair. These natives are too primitive to integrate; they throw spears! And now you think you are going be their self-appointed protector!

OLIVE: You make me sound simplistic.

HAROLD: I make it sound simple.

OLIVE: [*playing the downstage corridor*] What about the case about the Aboriginal woman raped by a white man—where is the justice?

HAROLD: [*moving downstage right*] So you've come all the way out here to save the women as well. Tell them to put some clothes on; don't give the men the wrong impression.

OLIVE: How can you say such disgusting things?

HAROLD: It is a disgusting place.

OLIVE: The rapist was then speared in his swag.

HAROLD: This place is too violent. No place to make a respectable life.

OLIVE: White people came and killed them all! Entire families slaughtered!

HAROLD: Yes, devastating. I'm sure there will be an investigation… But in the meantime let's get out of here.

OLIVE: After the massacres it was clear that killing Aboriginal people isn't a crime! Government investigations are complete shams. I will stay until I can see justice is served.

HAROLD: There is a process, Olive, it is a complicated process.

OLIVE: My heart lies with these people.

HAROLD: You will regret this.

OLIVE: Why? A place where the men are safe from exploitation, the women are safe from the disease-ridden soldiers and unsavoury pastoralists, and the children are safe to speak their language and be with their family.

HAROLD: Olive! Listen to what you are saying.

OLIVE: This is my fight.

HAROLD: Go home, this is no place for you; all your talents would be better used in Tasmania.

He crosses to OLIVE *and holds her from behind, and she holds herself.*

Paint the soft English lavender flowers along the lush Derwent River, not shrubs and weeds in rocks that scratch your skin. You and I are first and foremost artists. Gardeners.

OLIVE: I will fight for their rights.

HAROLD: [*on her right, level with her*] And I will be by your side, Olive, but this isn't the life for us.

OLIVE: Sometimes I want someone to listen and help me. I adore this place but… sometimes I feel like I am being held back.

HAROLD: [*looking at* OLIVE] What are you saying, Olive?

OLIVE: [*turning and looking at* HAROLD] How does one escape the past? Why did you leave me, Harold? And why the hell did you die! I can't forgive you.

HAROLD *exits upstage left.*

OLIVE *turns, strong, uncompromising.*

[*Addressing one audience member at a time*] The debate over land is fundamental to the expression of human rights. It is imperative we recognise the Aboriginals' right to land and that land management is consistent with cultural practices.

We could start by recognising that the land was theirs to begin with! When the British colonised the country in 1788 they considered it to be rightfully theirs. The British disregarded 40,000 years of habitation and the complex social, political and spiritual systems of the indigenous people, dismissing them as sub-human or savages. But the land was theirs. We took it.

I'm pushing for the political and economic will to start the process of land rights. The legal recognition of land ownership by Aboriginal people in conjunction with the customary land ownership systems. No compromises.

The path we walk upon reflects our future. I see two paths. One leads to the death of the oldest culture on the planet. The other leads to the strengthening of that culture. I can't compromise because I can't walk on two paths! It is simple!

I ask for justice and that we acknowledge a few simple truths: that we took the land, smashed their way of life, and completely undermined their entire existence. I am not alone; many people have come to the realisation that this issue must be addressed.

Yours sincerely, Olive M. Pink

TASMAN: [*offstage*] Miss Blue, Miss Blue!

> OLIVE *puts her hat on the table and grabs the rifle. She aims it at* TASMAN.

[*Offstage*] I'm not happy with you.

> TASMAN *enters, running, from stage right. He slides on his bum.*

OLIVE: Hello there. Do I know you?

> *She lowers the gun and returns it to the side of the table.*

TASMAN: You know me.

OLIVE: What's your name?

TASMAN: Tasman.

OLIVE: Tasman!

TASMAN: Yuwa Napaljarri. You come from Tasmania way. You name me.

OLIVE: Tasman.

TASMAN: You remember me, eh?

TASMAN *stands.*

OLIVE: You have grown!

TASMAN: You got shamed out bush.

OLIVE: I wasn't shamed.

TASMAN: You ran away.

OLIVE: I didn't run away.

TASMAN: You got penny, Miss Blue?

OLIVE: I wish I did, Tasman. I haven't got any money.

TASMAN: I guess I look somewhere else then, I get proper hungry in town. And you owe me. You careful of wrong way.

TASMAN *goes to exit towards upstage right.*

As TASMAN *scampers off* HENRY *enters upstage left, carrying a typewriter.* OLIVE *watches their exchange.*

HENRY: Excuse me.

TASMAN: Sorry, Mister. Hey, I never seen you before. Where you from?

HENRY: My name is Henry Wardlaw. You wouldn't happen to know if Miss Pink is around, would you?

TASMAN: Where'd you say you were from?

HENRY: Sydney.

TASMAN: That big place?

HENRY: Yes, it's a big place.

TASMAN: Big desert there.

HENRY: Something like that.

TASMAN: That lady likes the desert, she told me about Sydney.

HENRY: So where is Miss Pink?

TASMAN: Oh, Miss Blue? Yeah, she's over by the river. Say you got penny?

HENRY: No, I haven't got any money! Go away! And don't let me catch you annoying Miss Pink!

TASMAN: You can't tell me what to do.

TASMAN *exits upstage right.*

OLIVE: I'm here, Henry. Leave Tasman alone.

HENRY: [*stage right of the fire*] Looks like a troublemaker, if you ask me.

OLIVE: No-one asked you.

HENRY: That's sweet, but you must be careful.

OLIVE: I am careful.

HENRY: He is trouble.

OLIVE: What do you want?

HENRY: You get yourself in some tricky situations.

OLIVE: Why? Because I'm a woman.

HENRY: I did not mean that as an insult.

OLIVE: Just patronising.

HENRY: I just said that boy was trouble and you needed to take care. You are a single white woman living in an isolated place.

OLIVE: And you call yourself a free thinker.

HENRY: This is a dangerous place.

OLIVE: You are an upper-class city boy.

She crosses to HENRY *and adjusts his tie.*

I came to Alice Springs to fight for the common man, not to waste time with young city boys.

HENRY: And you fight with your friends.

OLIVE: In that case I don't need friendships.

HENRY: You don't mean that.

OLIVE: Tell me what I mean.

HENRY: Let's not argue. I am standing here with a gift.

OLIVE: Are you here to tempt me, Henry? Tell me what I can have and what I can't have?

HENRY: I am here to give you a typewriter.

OLIVE: I'm not sure if I can accept it.

HENRY: Why?

OLIVE: Because then I would feel obliged to you.

HENRY: Obliged?

OLIVE: I'd feel like I owed you something and I don't like owing people things. Besides, I am not sure on which side you stand, Henry.

HENRY: Which side?

OLIVE: Yes, what do you stand for? [*Crossing downstage left*] What would you give your life up for?

HENRY: I never thought about these things.

OLIVE: You should.

HENRY: Do you?

OLIVE: Of course. [*She reaches for her necklace.*] Every day.

HENRY: Here, it's to help you with your writing and research!

OLIVE: I am getting less interested in writing and research. [*Crossing downstage right*] I think more and more about creating a garden. I am first and foremost an artist and a nature lover.

HENRY: A garden! Miss Olive Pink, the nature lover?

OLIVE: Yes. For the future! Preserved for posterity and Alice Springs...

HENRY: Sound like a utopia!

OLIVE: My career as an anthropologist is over.

HENRY: My father mentioned you threw / in the towel.

OLIVE: Bothering anthropologists! Your father and his colleagues treat Aboriginal people as specimens, they are people.

HENRY: They blocked you.

OLIVE: Tribal secrets should not be published. They're secrets!

HENRY: I agree!

OLIVE: I only want to do things that are right. I'm going to create a garden.

HENRY: You want a garden?

OLIVE: I want to see this started before I die.

HENRY: Will you accept the typewriter, Miss Pink? It's a gift!

OLIVE: [*crossing downstage left*] I am suspicious of gifts.

HENRY: It's a gesture, then. Consider it a gesture from one friend to another.

OLIVE: I can't take the typewriter.

HENRY: Yes, you can.

OLIVE: Are you telling me what I can and cannot do?

HENRY: No, that isn't what I...

OLIVE: It isn't what you meant? Is that what you were saying? How does condescension feel when it's directed at you?

HENRY: I am not trying to be condescending. [*Crossing to the table*] I am putting the typewriter on the table and you can ignore it or do what you like with it.

OLIVE: I will accept the typewriter. But on one condition...

HENRY: What condition is that?

OLIVE: I owe you nothing.

HENRY: I would expect nothing less. I'll see you when I'm in Alice next.

OLIVE: When will that be?

HENRY: Could be up to six months.

OLIVE: I'll see you then.

> HENRY *exits upstage left.*

> *Music begins.*

> OLIVE *sits at the table, takes the lid off the typewriter and inserts paper. She puts on her glasses, places her hands on the keys and looks at the audience.*

> *The music ends.*

To the director of land and surveys, Mr Barclay and the assistant administrator Mr Marsh.

The beauty and view of Mount Gillen and the Todd gums is so lovely, especially in the morning. I ask could not the whole area and the two hills, like a horseshoe around it, be preserved for posterity as a place of peace and beauty for them.

The flat area has been denuded of most trees by the army, but also Aborigines and civilians at other times. So it is my unpaid duty, pleasure and honour to plant and develop it, so that it can in years to come be both of interest as showing what the arid regions grow naturally, and also be a place where future generations can sit under the trees and enjoy the view and plants in what is hoped will be a botanic gardens.

Yours truly, Olive M. Pink.

> HENRY *enters stage right.*

HENRY: I have some good news.

OLIVE: Have you?

> OLIVE *takes off her glasses, picks up her hat and crosses to the fire downstage left.*

HENRY: It is about this idea you have for a garden.

OLIVE: What is it?

HENRY: They have given it to you! Like you wished.

OLIVE: Don't joke.

HENRY: I wouldn't dare.

OLIVE: Hasluck did it? The Federal Minister said yes?

HENRY: Yes! It's yours.

OLIVE: They would not do that… would they? I will not accept.

HENRY: It's yours. This is your flora reserve. Or at least it is yours to work on, and there will be a wage.

OLIVE: Henry, this is outrageous. Henry, you are outrageous even offering me something like this.

HENRY: Outrageous good or outrageous bad!

OLIVE: This is very good.

HENRY: Miss Pink, the pay is not much and the land is damaged.

OLIVE: Oh, it's wonderful. This land needs protecting.

HENRY: It's not fenced.

OLIVE: It's beautiful.

HENRY: There's nothing out here.

OLIVE: [*looking upstage, indicating to Mount Gillen*] Look at those burning ranges. The caterpillars and that wild dog's nose…

HENRY: So you will take it?

OLIVE: I will think about it.

HENRY: You will need a house of some description.

Natasha Raja as Olive in the 2011 Alice Desert Festival production at the Olive Pink Botanic Garden in Alice Springs. (Photo: Steven Pearce)

OLIVE: I will build a hut. In the meantime I have my tent.

HENRY: Not that blasted tent!

OLIVE: [*moving to him*] You're so precious, Henry.

HENRY: I just want you to be comfortable... and... well... practical.

OLIVE: You are the nephew I never had.

HENRY: [*laughing in disbelief*] Ha! For this moment! I am glad this pleases you. I have arranged for some workers to build you a hut, which you will rent from the government, of course.

OLIVE: But I thought you said they were giving me the land.

HENRY: You wouldn't own the land. You would be a caretaker.

OLIVE: They would have me care for things I don't own?

HENRY: You have a number of friends. Friends in high places are petitioning the government. They will cover the expenses.

OLIVE: I don't trust people in high places. Does your father know you are here?

HENRY: What does my father have to do with this?

OLIVE: He is one of those people in high places desperate to shut me up. What are you doing here?

HENRY: I'm here trying to help.

OLIVE: Sounds too good to be true.

HENRY: Enjoy it.

OLIVE: I feel anxious.

HENRY: You are an enigma. I try to help and you refuse to accept help.

OLIVE: You give with one hand and take with the other. [*Crossing downstage centre*] Gardens are very different in Tasmania. I like it here.

HENRY: So you accept.

OLIVE: I will think about it.

> HENRY *crosses to the downstage right corner.*

[*Measured*] Out here, I've learnt to be wary. I see things more clearly now. We interfere with everything. Mostly we mistreat the locals, we treat them like slaves! I do not wish to remain a part of this.

It's our own failure. We simply cannot sweep injustice aside. Even if our own conscience [*holding her chest*] allowed us to in due course the world will not. There should be no mistake about this, our success in resolving these issues will have a significant bearing on our standing in the world.

Yours truly, Olive M. Pink.

Workers underscore music begins.

OLIVE *puts on her hat, crosses downstage right to* HENRY.

They are watching the workers.

How much do these men get per hour?

HENRY *doesn't answer.*

Henry, how much are these men earning?

HENRY *turns to her; he doesn't know how to respond.*

I want to know how much these men are earning. Are we cheating these men, Henry?

HENRY: They are cheap unskilled labour. They are earning what they get.

OLIVE: [*furiously*] They're getting below the award. I will not be a part of it!

HENRY: But…

OLIVE: I don't care if they are building me the Taj Mahal. One penny less than a white man's wage and they all walk!

HENRY: [*patronisingly*] They all walk? You're not going to organise these men, they have no concept of a wage. The Aboriginal wage is far below European. Employers calculate this on the value of the work.

OLIVE: You mean the value of the *worker*.

HENRY: Don't make this difficult. We are trying to build you a place to live.

OLIVE: I want these men to stop their work. [*To the workers; moving downstage centre*] You are being cheated. Go home. Do not come back until you are paid properly.

HENRY: I understand what you're saying, but / under these circumstances…

OLIVE: No buts! I will not have it.

HENRY: Why are you so angry? I am only trying to help. It is the way it is, I cannot change that… for the time being.

OLIVE: You are better than this.

HENRY: I thought I was the nephew you never had?

OLIVE: You were for a moment. Now you are just one of those people that get in my way. There is a long list. That bully Strehlow and your father top the list.

HENRY: You are turning your back on me like you turn your back on everyone / you have ever encountered.

OLIVE: I'm telling you what's right.

HENRY: I know what's right. We are on the same side.

OLIVE: Then do the right thing! You preach of human rights and subscribe to your socialist magazines and attend useless Left, progressive meetings, but what action do you take? What have you ever done?

HENRY: Look around you.

OLIVE: I see injustice!

HENRY: I see it, too.

OLIVE: I act on it! That's the difference between you and I. Social justice, equality, truth! Without action, these principles are just words, mere topics of conversation at a dinner party! I live it. It has cost me, Henry, and on no account will I lower my principles. Do not ask me to lower them… they are all I have.

HENRY: Your principles make building this hut impossible and relationships with government…

OLIVE: So what are you saying?

HENRY: [*invading her personal space*] I'm saying you could try to be a little accommodating.

OLIVE: [*not backing off*] Accommodating?

HENRY: You won't get anywhere if you fight with these people. Sometimes you have to give. You need support from a lot of people not just a few! Strength in numbers! United we bargain, divided we fall!

OLIVE: [*overlapping*] You are not listening. These men need to get paid properly. If you can't pay them, tell them to go home. I will not accept charity.

HENRY: [*backing off*] Your problem is you refuse to let people in. No-one can get too close to Miss Olive Muriel Pink.

OLIVE: [*shouting to the workers*] Go home! All of you… Go home.

>   *The music stops.*

I hate the government, I hate bureaucrats, and I hate fascists and racists and anthropologists. Call me Red, call me a commo, call me mad, say what you like, just go home. [*She ends up downstage centre. She takes a long, deep breath.*] Life is sitting on my chest—too much to be done… Too little energy to do them all. [*Calmly and quietly*] Henry, please get rid of them, just tell them… [*Pause.*] Sorry, there's no work here. Go home. All of you go home.

HENRY *exits upstage left.*

Underscored music begins.

OLIVE *takes off her hat.*

Here comes the nightsoil truck, and behind it the garbage truck. You can smell the former almost a block away and see the Aborigines perched on top. Naturally the *sanitary* workers are the *full bloods*, they being the most exploitable. They are being paid *two* pound a week, when the municipal section of the Northern Territory Administration states all mixed bloods, except the foreman, get the basic wage… The basic wage… is *five* pounds and 18 shillings per week.

They have no union. No hope. The treatment of these people makes me so angry.

The music ends.

Is it hopeless?

TASMAN *throws rocks from offstage right.*

OLIVE *grabs her rifle from against the table.*

Who is there? Come out. I will shoot.

TASMAN *enters stage right, running, but cautious.*

TASMAN: It's me! Don't shoot!
OLIVE: Who is me?
TASMAN: Tasman.
OLIVE: You. Why are you throwing stones?
TASMAN: You know why.
OLIVE: This makes me so angry.
TASMAN: Miss. I know what people say. They say you're mad. They say you do things the wrong way. You bad woman! I don't care about you.
OLIVE: So you throw stones at me.
TASMAN: You are a witch. You don't like half-castes! They say you are scary and mad. You know men's business.
OLIVE: Do I scare you?

TASMAN: *Yuwa*. You scare me! You too curious like all whitefellas. You know what I am talking about?

OLIVE: I suppose I do. [*She goes into her tent to get an orange.*] Now you take this.

> *She hands him the orange. He looks at the fruit with disdain.* HAROLD *moves down from upstage left.*

Take it and run away. Please. I'm sorry I have nothing else to give.

TASMAN: So you just like to take.

OLIVE: No I don't / yes, maybe I do.

TASMAN: *Yuwa*. You are right about that. I gonna make a big trouble.

> TASMAN *takes the fruit, throws it over the audience and runs off upstage right.*

> OLIVE *crosses to the tent and begins to untie it.* HAROLD *unties the other side. They only reveal the hut verandah.*

HAROLD: Don't let him get away with that.

OLIVE: I'm to blame.

HAROLD: You should just leave this place.

OLIVE: No, I will not. I can't.

HAROLD: What are you doing here? Why don't you go home?

OLIVE: Where?

HAROLD: Tasmania.

OLIVE: Tasmania is no longer home.

HAROLD: Sydney, Perth, go to Timbuktu. Anywhere but this place.

OLIVE: I can't.

HAROLD: You can. What can one woman do out here?

OLIVE: I can do so much.

HAROLD: You are not supported here.

OLIVE: I have my supporters.

HAROLD: You should own this land.

OLIVE: I'm here to take care of it.

HAROLD: You are not making sense.

OLIVE: I need this place.

> OLIVE *enters the tent and changes into overalls.*

> HAROLD *crosses downstage left. Squats and watches.*

> *Johnny's theme music begins.*

Wearing only trousers, JOHNNY *enters upstage left and stops downstage centre.*

The music ends.

JOHNNY: [*indirectly addressing the audience*] Miss Pink went to Chilla Well. Aboriginal people brought her to Chilla Well. They gave her goanna to eat and kangaroo. They took her digging for bush yams— they are big like potato. They told her everything. She really like them witchetty grubs. That Napaljarri grow up a whole mob of *yapa,* giving them clothes, flour, corned beef, sugar and tea—Miss Pink don't like other whites. Only *yapa.* She was always giving whitefellas a piece of her mind... She taught how to make clothes. She was showing them how to put pants on. She was telling them to cover the *lampunu* [breasts] and told them what *lampunu* meant to whitefellas. [*Turning upstage, calling to the tent*] Napaljarri!

OLIVE: [*from the tent*] Yes?

OLIVE *comes out of the tent, dressed in overalls.*

JOHNNY: My name is Johnny; we met at Mount Doreen.

OLIVE: Tjampitjinpa?

JOHNNY: *Yuwa.* My brother just passed away, he was the last one left.

OLIVE *goes to touch him, but doesn't.*

OLIVE: I'm so sorry to hear that.

JOHNNY: You were standing up for us.

OLIVE: It was devastating.

JOHNNY: I still can't work out why it happened.

OLIVE: White ignorance and white prejudice.

JOHNNY: Can you do something for me?

OLIVE: What?

JOHNNY: I need to know why these bad things are happening. Whitefellas take over. Cattle take over. Lots of *yapa* dying, but you are different. You fight for us.

OLIVE: Not very well.

JOHNNY: I don't know much about white man's politics but you can teach me. I'll fight. Just teach me.

OLIVE: I do need someone to help me build a hut and a garden.

HAROLD: No, Olive.

HAROLD *crosses upstage of* OLIVE.

JOHNNY: I can do that. But I want you to teach me how white people think. I want to learn about white man's thinking.

OLIVE: You help me build a hut and a garden. I will teach you about us.

JOHNNY: What place is this?

JOHNNY *moves downstage centre.*

HAROLD: I don't like the look of him.

JOHNNY: Does this place belong to you?

OLIVE: It's not my land. It's government land.

JOHNNY: They just give him to you? Just like that? I didn't know that government mob gave away land, I thought they just took him.

OLIVE: I have dreams for this place.

JOHNNY: Nobody own land.

OLIVE: [*moving to the tent*] I'm beginning to wonder… was the land given to me, [*getting a shovel*] or was I given to the land?

She tries to hand JOHNNY *the shovel.*

You will receive the full wage. Let's start work.

JOHNNY: Not too fast, Napaljarri. Slowly. Too hot!

JOHNNY *crosses to the tent.*

HAROLD: Tell him to go.

JOHNNY: If you belong to the land, you realise the land owns you.

JOHNNY *enters the tent.*

HAROLD: You are not really attempting to grow anything here. Not with him.

OLIVE: Yes we are, Harold.

HAROLD: Look at this soil… this… [*squatting and throwing up dirt*] sand!

OLIVE: We will grow vegetables and flowers. [*Kneeling at the plant rows*] Carnations.

HAROLD: When was the last time it rained?

OLIVE: I'm not sure.

HAROLD: [*opposite* OLIVE, *at a plant row*] Will it rain?

OLIVE: I'm happy sitting here planting my favourite Sturt Bean Tree.

HAROLD: [*squatting opposite* OLIVE] That's a Bat's Wing Coral Tree; otherwise called Erythrina vespertilio.

OLIVE: Lovely, when it blossoms.

HAROLD: Do you remember my garden? Sketching? I'd watch you for hours. You're a wonderful artist, such a perfectionist.

OLIVE: I have things to do here.

HAROLD: [*standing*] I hate the thought of you working with that man.

OLIVE *stands and looks at* HAROLD.

OLIVE: You left and died.

HAROLD: It was my duty. I'm sorry.

Heat music underscore.

JOHNNY *comes out of the tent, wearing a shirt and overalls. He reveals the hut then crosses to plant row one and digs.*

OLIVE: [*to the audience, light, joyous, no pauses*] In my garden I have rockmelons. I had tomatoes, they're mostly diseased now. I have carnations, which I hope to later make money out of, as well as chrysanthemums and gladioli. I don't think I could sell bulbs, certainly not my white hyacinths. I have 18 flourishing gum trees and the yucca is in blossom. Lovely! There are two autumn crocuses in bud. Michaelmas daisies and mignonette in flower and lots of other plants growing well in eight-gallon drums and plenty of native bluebells that I transplanted from the Todd River bank. They are heavenly, I adore them. But not most blue flowers—white, mauve and pale yellow are my favourites. I love working on the garden, it's the most beautiful spot in Alice Springs. A peace and beauty spot for future generations.

[*To* JOHNNY] Can you please dig the trench along here? [*Indicating plant row three*] The water must flow right down to the end.

JOHNNY: [*working at plant row one*] *Yuwa.*

OLIVE: *Purdarnkajurlu* [Listen to me], when you have finished that would you mind doing the same along this row, please.

She indicates plant row two.

JOHNNY: I know what to do.

OLIVE: Yes, but please, it's my garden.

JOHNNY: You want to talk about respect?

OLIVE: I treat people with respect.

JOHNNY: Little bit of language and you think you know.

OLIVE: I don't mean to sound like that.

OLIVE *enters the hut.*

JOHNNY: [*leaning on his shovel at plant row one*] Walpiri people don't need to talk respectful words because respect is already there… from birth! Our kids are going to school and the first thing they've got to learn is whitefella manners. Our kids can say them words… but I don't think they really know. White man go around and take children from their mothers! They steal them because they've got a little bit of white skin. Put them in a mission to teach 'em English and *respect*? We've got no manners? No respect? I'll tell you, the way we get treated I don't see any respect! Even if they do say 'please'!

He continues to dig.

OLIVE *storms out of the hut, grabs the rifle.*

OLIVE: [*aiming the rifle*] Are those children back? Don't bother throwing rocks at my hut! I'll shoot!

JOHNNY: Now you got a rifle there is no use for words like 'please'!

OLIVE: Please? I treat people with respect.

OLIVE *puts down the rifle.*

JOHNNY: Respect in my culture lies in action, not words.

OLIVE: I see. [*Crossing to plant row three*] I asked you please shovel that dirt here!

JOHNNY: I put it here, please?

OLIVE: Not there. Here, here!

JOHNNY: I know where the dirt should go; that's where I'll put him, thank you.

OLIVE: Are you trying to tell me something?

JOHNNY: I got respect for you, it's already there. I don't need manners.

OLIVE *takes up a watering can. As she waters some plants,* JOHNNY *kneels to plant a tree.*

OLIVE: I'll try to remember that.

JOHNNY: I speak English, that doesn't make me English. [*Watching her watering*] Why do you do that? Why do you water some plants and not others?

OLIVE: You will laugh at me.

JOHNNY: I've been laughing at you for some time now, Napaljarri.

HAROLD *moves between* OLIVE *and* JOHNNY, *slightly upstage of them.*

HAROLD: He has no manners.

OLIVE: You wouldn't be the first to call me crazy.

JOHNNY: Why do white men not recognise us as equal? They treat us like we're less.

OLIVE: They don't consider you. They want your land.

She kneels opposite JOHNNY.

HAROLD: It's our land. We came here and did something with it.

JOHNNY: Like the garden? You don't own it.

OLIVE: I don't own it.

JOHNNY: Government owns it.

OLIVE: That's right.

JOHNNY: Same government owns our country.

OLIVE: That is what they say.

HAROLD: I don't like him. He can't look after himself.

OLIVE: You are different.

HAROLD: Why are you wasting time with him?

JOHNNY: That's not an answer.

HAROLD: He is primitive. He can't understand all this!

JOHNNY: They might be frightened or suspicious of us, but hate us? They don't even know us.

OLIVE: It's easier to get rid of something you don't like, rather than something you do.

JOHNNY: They just want to get rid of us.

OLIVE: You've got what they want.

JOHNNY: Waterholes?

OLIVE: [*standing, leaving the watering can*] No. Land, Johnny. They want it and Aboriginals are on it. I try to make people grasp this. I want the entire country to know what has happened here.

JOHNNY: [*back to planting*] Seems like a bloody waste of time if no-one is listening to what you got to say.

OLIVE: Standing up for what you believe in is never a waste of time! And if we shout loud enough they'll listen.

JOHNNY: Maybe they will. But they won't care, because we're different.

OLIVE: They don't respect you.

JOHNNY: That's right.

OLIVE: Are you saying we need to tell them not what is happening to your people, but who you are?

JOHNNY: *Yuwa.*

HAROLD: Can you see what this place has done to you? [*Moving upstage*] When those savages told you their secrets they cursed you as well. Let's make our own garden. I like a different sort of garden. You are wasting your time in this place with this man.

> HAROLD *exits upstage left.*

OLIVE: [*moving downstage centre*] Dear sir.

Imagine that you are sitting near the little campfires of a lot of black fellows and asking them their views. Imagine, as I have seen it, a sky full of stars that one finds it hard to believe that it is the same old sky we have in the south, so parsimonious is the sprinkling of them there by comparison.

We need to think *with* Aborigines, instead of just *for* the Aborigines. And it is only by thinking with them that we shall ever have sympathetic insight to the injustice we have done to them.

Yours sincerely, Olive M. Pink.

She crosses to plant row one.

I name them.

JOHNNY: [*following on the other side of the row*] You name the plants?

OLIVE: Yes. These plants are becoming more real to me every day, they are like people. Each one of these red river gums has a name. Some I name after people I like, others are named after people who have fallen out of favour and so I treat the plants accordingly. [*Starting at the downstage end of a plant row*] This tree is Mr Ted Egan and now this one is John Blakeman, that is Reg Harris, over there is Tom Day and my favourite is Henry Wardlaw. [*Pointing at the upstage plant, sternly*] This is Mr Braitling. I'm not watering you anymore!

JOHNNY: You think plants are like people?

OLIVE: I agree it is a little strange.

JOHNNY: We think plants are like people too.

OLIVE: They're just as important!

JOHNNY: We are part of the land. Plants nourish us. We all nourish the land.

OLIVE: We are starting to think alike.

JOHNNY: [*playing fourth wall*] *Yuwa*. If the people are sick, the land is sick.

OLIVE: I see.

JOHNNY: We are both far from home.

OLIVE: Yes, Johnny, we are.

JOHNNY: Cuppa tea?

> JOHNNY *moves to stage right of the fire.*

> OLIVE *enters the hut and returns holding a tray with two pannikins, a tin of sugar cubes and tongs. She sits downstage left of the fire and pours them tea.*

OLIVE: No rain for so long now. We have to save water. Baths and watering, I miss the joy of both.

> *She puts one cube of sugar in Johnny's pannikin.* JOHNNY *indicates more.* OLIVE *puts two more cubes in.*

This is good wood, burns long and slow.

JOHNNY: *Yuwa!* I told you. Hey, woman, tell me that story.

OLIVE: You always ask for that story, Johnny.

JOHNNY: [*nodding*] Hmm.

OLIVE: Okay, I'll tell you. We made that deal.

JOHNNY: You and I will build this garden.

OLIVE: [*noticing a rabbit upstage right*] That's right, Johnny. The world began with a garden, simple and honest; I hope that's how it ends.

> *She slowly gets her rifle. Moving upstage of the hut, she aims and shoots, then puts the rifle back.*

Rabbit for dinner, Johnny.

JOHNNY: You are crazy, Napaljarri. *Yuwow!*

> JOHNNY *exits upstage right.*

OLIVE: [*with tea, to the audience*] I went to Reg Harris's house for tea the other day. He arrived unannounced and insisted I sit in his car. He then drove me into town, so many things have changed in the last 18 months, including the hospital. They have a lovely home, which is filled with… things, many things. I asked his wife to show me around. We came across this woman in the bedroom. 'Why haven't

I been introduced to this lady' I demanded to know. To which, Mrs Harris, bless her, replied, 'Miss Pink, that is not another lady but your own reflection in a full-length mirror'. [*She laughs.*] I don't own a mirror; I haven't owned a mirror in… decades! But to think I didn't recognise myself!

She touches her face again.

TASMAN *enters upstage left, running; he's looking back to see if he's being chased.*

Tasman! What are you doing, young man?

TASMAN: None of your business.

OLIVE: You will get in trouble.

TASMAN: You are just a stupid white lady. I'm not listening to you.

OLIVE: They will lock you up.

TASMAN: I don't care.

OLIVE: You won't get away with it.

TASMAN: I don't care!

OLIVE: You have to treat people and their property with respect.

TASMAN: Why? They don't treat me with respect.

OLIVE: I will get Johnny. He will sort you out.

TASMAN: I don't care what he has to say. He can't tell me what to do!

TASMAN *exits upstage right.*

Music begins.

OLIVE *crosses to the fire. She picks up Johnny's pannikin, then hers, and places them on the tray and takes it into the hut.*

OLIVE *returns to stoke the fire.*

The music fades out.

HENRY: [*offstage*] Hello!

HENRY *enters upstage left with a package for her.*

Hello! I have something for you.

HENRY *gives* OLIVE *the package. She opens it.*

OLIVE: Books. [*She is pleased.*] Literature! Charles Bean. I cannot afford books anymore and the town library is pathetic. Johnny, come see.

JOHNNY *enters upstage right, carrying a stew pot, which he places on the fire. He looks at the books.*

JOHNNY: These are good.

OLIVE: They are. This is generous.

HENRY: It's no trouble. My wife sends her regards.

OLIVE: How is she? Is her rationale to give me the things I like, so I will be too busy to speak out and so not be an embarrassment?! Is that it?

HENRY: You are very feisty today.

OLIVE: I'll take them, Johnny and I will read them together.

She places the books on the table.

HENRY: Glad to hear it.

OLIVE: Sometimes I'm not sure if I'm teaching him or if he's teaching me?

HENRY: I have some unfortunate news.

OLIVE: In that case can I offer you some sherry? Cake?

HENRY: That would be lovely; I don't want to take up too much of your time.

OLIVE: Neither do I!

OLIVE enters the hut.

JOHNNY stirs the stew.

HENRY: What's for dinner, Johnny?

JOHNNY: Rabbit.

HENRY: Good, makes a nice change from Weet-Bix.

They laugh.

JOHNNY: *Yuwa*, Napaljarri, love them Weet-Bix!

OLIVE exits the hut, carrying a glass of sherry and a piece of cake on a china plate. She stands stage left of the fire.

OLIVE: Don't you start, Henry! [*To* JOHNNY] Whose side are you on? [*To* HENRY] Now give me the bad news.

HENRY: Tasman is in prison.

JOHNNY: [*standing*] What for?

HENRY: Theft.

OLIVE: Did he do it?

HENRY: I don't know.

JOHNNY: It doesn't matter.

HENRY: There's no proof, his word against theirs.

OLIVE: I will have a word with Ted. He will know. What did he steal?

HENRY: It won't matter.

JOHNNY: [*moving downstage right*] Why does this keep happening to us?

OLIVE: I must visit him tomorrow.

JOHNNY: I am sick of this.

OLIVE: I'll take some fruit.

JOHNNY: Oh, that'll help…

HENRY: That will be helpful.

> JOHNNY *growls with frustration and anger.*

JOHNNY: I can't do anything.

OLIVE: I'll write to the minister.

JOHNNY: They can't either. All they do is talk.

HENRY: Reverend McKay?

OLIVE: Who?

HENRY: Fred.

JOHNNY: I need to think about this.

OLIVE: Who knows what they're feeding him. I'll take biscuits.

JOHNNY: [*playing fourth wall*] It won't be goanna… Might be schnitzel, I've had schnitzel!

HENRY: It won't be schnitzel.

> *He downs the sherry, coughs, and hands the glass back to* OLIVE.

Thanks for the drop. Awful as always. That works a treat, giving your guests bad sherry to ensure the visit is quick!

OLIVE: You know too much for my liking. [*Placing the glass and plate on the table*] I'll take fruit and find out Tasman's version of events.

JOHNNY: That jail fella hates you, Napaljarri. He won't let you in. Can you help us?

OLIVE: I have strong opinions. And I will share these with him tomorrow.

HENRY: I'll follow up on this. Leave it with me.

OLIVE: Oh! You have finally developed a backbone?

HENRY: I can communicate with the officers.

OLIVE: And I can't?

HENRY: Your tactics don't work. People don't respond to your ranting and raving.

OLIVE: I beg your pardon?

HENRY: We have different methods of attack! I can handle this!

OLIVE: How clever of you, I'll see you to the gate. I need to check it.

> OLIVE *exits behind the hut.* HENRY *exits behind the hut, then upstage left.*

HENRY: See you, Johnny.

JOHNNY: Thank you, please, and good luck. Get that young fella out of jail… And you're welcome.

JOHNNY: [*moving downstage centre*] I come from the North West. [*He points.*] There are different spirits here. I can see them shapes. This is another man's country.

Aboriginal culture is older than all those other whitefellas. But they don't respect this. They shoot first and lock people up. Then they say please. I'm not anti-whitefella but they don't respect my custom and tradition here.

What am I doing here? I'm working on drainage and irrigation and building a garden. And still that fella Tasman is in jail. Nothing changes. I got to do something about this ignorance and prejudice.

> JOHNNY *exits stage left.*

> *Romantic music underscore.*

> HAROLD *enters stage right.*

HAROLD: Mrs Olive Southern.

> OLIVE *enters from behind the hut to the centre of the stage, wearing her skirt and blouse.*

OLIVE: Mrs Olive Southern. Mrs Olive Muriel Southern. Mrs Olive Muriel Pink… Southern?… No! Olive Muriel Pink.

> HAROLD *moves down to her.*

HAROLD: How different our lives would have been.

OLIVE: [*to the audience, moving downstage centre*] We planned to marry, the war came and Harold enlisted. When Harold left, my mother and I settled in Sydney. One moment I was a girl in an obscure little town. The next I was a woman in the city. I volunteered for the Red Cross to meet the hospital ships coming back from the war. I qualified for a Town Planning Diploma at the University of Sydney. I was so happy.

Till the news came.

Captain Harold Southern, of the 16th Battalion, has died leading his men into battle at Gallipoli. My heart broke: the doctors diagnosed a strained valve and a weak heart and prescribed a tonic.

Once peace returned I found myself among an active, intellectual and unconventional group of unmarried men and women...

To this day I drink that sour tonic.

HAROLD: I'm still here with you.

The romantic music fades out.

OLIVE: I want to be alone to soak up the solitude and the glorious sky and to write my notes and letters.

OLIVE *goes into the hut.*

JOHNNY *enters from behind the hut.*

JOHNNY: Who the hell are you?

HAROLD: I want you to leave.

JOHNNY: I'm helping her.

HAROLD: You are wasting her time.

JOHNNY *looks around in disbelief.*

JOHNNY: You're a ghost!

HAROLD: I'm an angel.

JOHNNY: A guardian angel?

HAROLD: Yes I am.

JOHNNY: You don't look like an angel.

HAROLD: What is an angel supposed to look like?

JOHNNY: [*to himself, playing fourth wall*] Too hot. I must be seeing things.

HAROLD: You are seeing right. I'm here.

JOHNNY: Okay, if you are an angel, who are you guarding?

HAROLD: Her.

JOHNNY: Are you her husband?

HAROLD: I love her.

JOHNNY: So you will look after her?

HAROLD: Better than you could.

JOHNNY: [*looking towards the hut*] I need to know that she will be safe.

HAROLD: I'd never let anything happen to her.

JOHNNY: It's up to you now. This is an unforgiving country.

HAROLD: I promise.

JOHNNY: I'll check up on that woman.

HAROLD: I'll keep an eye on her, Johnny. [*Crossing to the hut, downstage left corner*] You can go now.

> JOHNNY *moves upstage, stops, turns, squats and watches from a distance.*

> *Music.*

> OLIVE *storms out of the hut, furious. She stands behind the typewriter.*

> *The music fades out.*

OLIVE: [*addressing the audience and typewriter*] Dear sir.

I saw a Warden has been sent to protect mining rights!— But what about the rights of our black fellow humans? I am sure they are not being protected. Why wasn't I born a man when I want to do the things they do and my bothering sex blocks me.

Yours sincerely, Olive M. Pink.

> *She happily moves downstage centre.*

Dear sir.

Occasionally, something wonderful takes place. I met a young painter, Albert Namatjira. He is a beginner but a brilliant one— in his simplicity of treatment of the subject. I bought two of his works. Those I have, have a spiritual quality.

Yours truly, Olive M. Pin—

> *She looks off right, very angry.*

> *Plane music.*

What is that?! Those damned firemen next door! I've had it! I will no longer put up with this harassment, this time they have gone too far!

HAROLD: There, there, my love.

OLIVE: They steal my oranges, play their music well into the late hours of the night! Curse at me and blast me with their engine hose, and in a time of drought?!

HAROLD: Don't let them get you down.

> *The plane music is louder, closer.*

> OLIVE *wildly screams at the plane.*

OLIVE: Can't you leave an old lady alone, you bureaucratic bully…!

> HAROLD *hands the rifle to* OLIVE.

You Roman Catholic fascist! Pastoralist pervert!

> OLIVE *fires the rifle at the plane.*

HAROLD: Good shot, old girl. That's the spirit. I'll protect you now.

OLIVE: [*playing fourth wall*] Harold.

HAROLD: Yes?

OLIVE: You are everything to me. What you gave up influences everything I do. I stand for truth, honour, justice and beauty. You taught me that, above all else. It keeps me going. It sustains me!

HAROLD: And you sustain me.

OLIVE: [*looking at* HAROLD] I know, but now I want you to leave.

> OLIVE *hands back the rifle.*

HAROLD: [*arcing upstage*] My parents warned me that you would be a handful. You have been! Aahh, but what a soul! What a beauty!

> HAROLD *returns the rifle to the side of the table.*

OLIVE: I was young and… beautiful.

> OLIVE *explores her face and neck with her hands.*

> JOHNNY *stands, quietly, watching. He starts moving down to her.*

HAROLD: To me fair friend, you never can be old,
> For as you were when first your eye I ey'd,
> Such seems your beauty still.

> OLIVE *swoons and falls on the floor.* JOHNNY *rushes and holds her. She slowly awakens.*

She needs her tonic. Get her the tonic!

> HAROLD *backs upstage left, helpless.*

OLIVE: I need some water, Johnny.

> JOHNNY *gets water from the table and gives it to her. He helps her stand slowly.*

I was in love with you, Harold, but now my heart belongs here.

> JOHNNY *takes her into the hut.*

> HAROLD *exits upstage left.*

Music starts.

JOHNNY *enters from the hut to stoke the fire.*

OLIVE *exits the hut, carrying a basket of flowers. She is wearing her jacket and town hat. It's a heated debate.*

The music fades out.

I'm going.

JOHNNY: [*standing*] Where are you going?

OLIVE: That superintendent doesn't let me visit. What's he hiding in there? I will go to jail to find out.

JOHNNY: You just like to fight.

OLIVE: [*crossing to* JOHNNY] I need to see first-hand. If they don't let me in they can lock me up.

JOHNNY: They will lock you up.

OLIVE: I want them to.

JOHNNY: Not good being locked up.

OLIVE: The penalty is a fine or one day in jail. I've chosen jail.

HENRY *enters upstage left.*

HENRY: He paid your fine.

OLIVE: What? But I want to go to jail.

HENRY: The jailer paid your fine, so you will not be imprisoned.

JOHNNY: What happened?

OLIVE: That jailer pig… paid my fine.

HENRY: No jail for you.

HENRY *exits upstage left.*

JOHNNY *laughs until he starts coughing and then spits on the ground.*

OLIVE *returns the flowers to the hut.*

OLIVE: Are you okay?

JOHNNY: I'm sick.

OLIVE: Have you been using that rubbing medicine?

JOHNNY: No. I need to go home. Be in my father's country. Teach them young fellas.

OLIVE: What about our garden?

JOHNNY: I have to go.

OLIVE: But what about our garden?

JOHNNY: I helped you build your hut and the garden. This was never our land.

OLIVE *and* JOHNNY *stand side by side in front of the fire.*

OLIVE: No.

JOHNNY: Not ours.

OLIVE: It never was ours.

JOHNNY: We only tried to make him better.

OLIVE: Have we made it better? I no longer know.

JOHNNY: You will be alright.

OLIVE: I don't need looking after.

JOHNNY: You have people who will take care of you.

OLIVE: I've always taken care of myself.

JOHNNY: I need my people to take care of me.

OLIVE: You need to take care of your people. I understand.

JOHNNY: What about this?

OLIVE: Let's get these ridiculous carnations out of the ground, they don't belong here anyway. [*She crosses upstage centre and pulls out carnations from an eight-gallon drum.*] Are you going to work today, Johnny, or are you too sick of this place?

JOHNNY: *Yuwa.*

He moves upstage of plant row three.

OLIVE: I am not growing foreign plants anymore. This is what I want. Native plants and trees.

JOHNNY *picks up his shovel. He begins working on the pile of dirt.*

OLIVE *moves downstage of the plant row.*

[*Playing fourth wall*] Something happened out bush. It was hot. No food. I was hungry. I couldn't sleep… I walked out of my hut and into the camp. I heard something. I have never told anyone.

JOHNNY *stops walking.*

There were people. I shouldn't have. I followed the sound and in the darkness… Secret. I wasn't invited. I know.

JOHNNY: You stayed?

OLIVE: I should have known better.

JOHNNY: Did you stay?

OLIVE: I'm ashamed. The next day the man came to me. He'd seen me. He yelled. Attacked me. I tried to get back to my camp, my rifle. I tripped. He hit the back of my head, my hands clasped behind my head—my plait and collar and veil—blood. And a weak boomerang saved my life. I won't speak of it again. [*She picks up the flowers she has just pulled out.*] The money for these flowers will pay for a new rake. [*She picks up the basket.*] These I will give to young Josie, she's getting married.

OLIVE *puts the flowers on the porch.*

JOHNNY: I've gotta go to my country.

He crosses to stage right of the fire.

OLIVE: What?

JOHNNY: I got to help *yapa.*

OLIVE: You can't.

JOHNNY: Teach them young fellas.

OLIVE: So it's time to say goodbye?

She stands centre stage with JOHNNY.

JOHNNY: Goodbye is hard.

OLIVE: I'll miss you.

She touches his arm.

JOHNNY: I've got to go.

OLIVE: Thank you for this garden.

JOHNNY: Look after 'im.

OLIVE: I will.

Johnny's theme music comes in.

JOHNNY *exits upstage left.*

OLIVE *crosses downstage centre as the music fades out.*

[*To the audience*] Ever so gradually I am seeing Australia through Aboriginal eyes. Johnny, you make me see how much we have lost by living apart. If an Aboriginal man is without his land he is without his soul. It's not a question of ownership, it's something else. It's about the responsibility of looking after the land. I no longer believe the land is to own but to look after; it is the very essence of being. Connection is much deeper, much more complex. To be away from your home is to be without substance.

OLIVE *enters the hut.*

Cold music comes in: it's a cold winter's evening.

OLIVE *comes out of the hut, crossing downstage centre in front of the fire. She is barefoot, wearing a white nightdress, wrapped in a blanket, and carrying a bucket of water.*

The cold music fades out.

My God, it's freezing. Each winter feels colder then the last. The icy wind has settled into my bones. I feel like a lizard in need of sun. Then summer arrives, a burning hell. [*She drops the blanket.*] I could not bear another summer. [*She tips the bucket of water over herself.*] Harold, are you here?

HAROLD *enters upstage right, holding a lit candle.*

HAROLD: [*moving downstage to her*] I'm here, darling, are you ready? I waited.

OLIVE: I'm ready. Over time I begin to fit in here. I learned to realise I am in Aranda country. I have found comfort here. The old men call me Corkwood Honey. My resting place will be here beneath these caterpillar ranges. Underneath and above. I am in Aranda country.

HAROLD: You've made it your home.

OLIVE: How I begged you to stop haunting me, now you're all I ask for.

HAROLD: This is it, old girl.

OLIVE: Harold, I feel so strange, I feel powerful. For once I have complete control over my life, ironically on the day of my death. Oh, my beautiful garden, I wouldn't rather be anywhere else. This earth, I'll always belong to you.

OLIVE *lays on the ground.*

HAROLD *blows out the candle and stays still.*

Gentle music comes in.

TASMAN *enters upstage right. He slowly walks to* OLIVE, *stopping stage centre, upstage of her.*

TASMAN: Some friends found Napaljarri in the cold that night and called that ambulance, she didn't pass away on this land like she wished.

But she did wake up enough to swear at them ambulance men before they took her away. Then she died.

He places the blanket over OLIVE*'s body.*

She organised and paid for her funeral and her gravestone. You can't miss 'im in the cemetery; it's the only one facing wrong way, looking straight up at Mount Gillen.

The gentle music fades out.

Post show music comes in.

THE END

www.ingramcontent.com/pod-product-compliance
Lightning Source LLC
Chambersburg PA
CBHW041935090426
42744CB00017B/2071